A DIALECTIC APPROACH TO CRIMINAL LAW

A DIALECTIC APPROACH TO CRIMINAL LAW

Dr. Michael Dassama

Copyright © 2020 by Dr. Michael Dassama.

ISBN:	Softcover	978-1-9845-9341-2
	eBook	978-1-9845-9340-5

All rights reserved. No part of this book may be reproduced or transmitted in any form or by any means, electronic or mechanical, including photocopying, recording, or by any information storage and retrieval system, without permission in writing from the copyright owner.

Any people depicted in stock imagery provided by Getty Images are models, and such images are being used for illustrative purposes only.
Certain stock imagery © Getty Images.

Print information available on the last page.

Rev. date: 01/21/2020

To order additional copies of this book, contact:
Xlibris
800-056-3182
www.Xlibrispublishing.co.uk
Orders@Xlibrispublishing.co.uk
808441

PREFACE

The study of criminal law is interesting and quite challenging as it broadens intellectual horizon and, makes receptivity more subjective on the basis of its variant course patterns in which, it is structured. Because it is based on every day happenings in which it tend to depict, both the state and the individual in relation to offences. Criminal law has always attracted academic interest of students of law than most other areas of law disciplines in institutions of learning; due to its dynamic importance in the labour market for easy job prospects. It is common place to emphasise that, criminal lawyers tend to be more socially vibrant and highly engaging when it comes to court attendance in juxtaposition to other disciplines in law.

Due to the enormity of criminal cases, pressure tends to be mounted on both the crown prosecution service which is a, state apprentices in conjunction with litigants. What should be noted is, differences in criminal interpretations within geo-political boundaries does not defaced the reality of importance of criminal law because, the protection of people and society against lawlessness, is common placed which cannot be deluded. In this regard, it is my intention in this book to create awareness and to establish relativity of common ground in the understanding of criminal law. Although many text books and other reading materials have been written and published on criminal law yet, the complexity of style and presentation of material facts, has in many ways, left students in a state of bewilderment due to the 'crab nature' in which some of those texts were written. The primary aim of this exercise is to present a user friendly text which will not, only assist students in the understanding of criminal law as it ought to be but also, to have confident in themselves in relation to the subject matter.

Students are usually in the habit of excessively memorizing legal texts which in most cases are, responsible for brain fag or failure in complex examination situation thus culminating to unsatisfactory examination results. In addressing this all important critical problem, it is my intention to present this book in easy readable version with, simplified case law to enhance better and comprehensive understanding of every argument as much as possible. In this regard, it is my expectation that materials in this book, could enhanced students with the opportunity of an in- depth knowledge of the subject matter both for examination purpose and as well as, for professional recapitulation exercises.

Over the years, students of law have had difficulty in assimilating law texts because of the 'higgledy-piggledy' conceptual nature in which, most of those books have been written. A disheartening confrontation of such challenges which presents itself to students has been by-and-large, culminated to frustration and possible change of discipline. The situational circumstances which, had bedevilled students for such protraction of time, had gingered the production of this book with the intention of, easing anxiety and mental perturbation.

It is not sufficient an idea to rely on just one text book for the study of criminal law because, variety of ideas from different text books, will not only provide students with multiple content based knowledge to study criminal law but also, enhances students with recapitulation exercises in dealing with complex case studies. Although it is essential to note that, materials which constitute the completion of this book project, are found in almost all text books related to the study of law within this dimension yet, the simplistic and flexible pattern adopted to enhance assimilation of material facts, makes all the difference.

Since it is not literally possible to cover all cases related to this field, it is therefore essential for students, to endeavour extra research into current case law through electronic media and major news papers where some of these cases could be easily accessed. It is extremely important for current cases to be enshrined within legal presentation especially where, such matter requires codification and analysis. Students are also advised to use other text books and any related material to enhance better understanding of the subject and at the same time, be able to juxtapose various arguments and thus, to objectively surmised relevant points for perusal. It is against this background that, students will be gearing their interest in criminal law which this book, tend to provide especially where complex and crabby phrases are put in simplistic format for easy understanding.

Over the years as lecturer of this subject, in various colleges in London, United Kingdom, my observation has been the inability of most students to paraphrase legal arguments especially in examination condition within the scope of limited, allotted time frame. In this regard, outcome of examination result tend to be, unsatisfactory and highly very disappointing due to the rambling and inconsistencies that most examination scripts, tend to have.

The aim of this text is to overcome those shortcomings and pitfalls so that students will have a better understanding how to maximise their time in exams condition by applying requisite skills and knowledge provided in this book project. It should be noted that those student, who uses time and material facts objectively tend to do well than those who, randomly rumbled in exams condition. Precision and much clarity in answering questions, could be a bench-mark in examination success as it encourages examiners to concentrate on the trends of arguments that is expostulated in answering respective questions than those who may be in the bad habit of, using elaborately and undulating expressions that could be a bit verbose and highly distasteful in the eyes of examiners.

In this regard, it is my desire to making necessary inputs which may serve as springboard in this book project, capable of motivating and at the same time, providing guidelines to answering questions under examination tension by, presenting synopsis in most case law for qualitative precision.

For this purpose, it is intended to divide the book into two parts of which part **one** will be looking at probability testing, analysis and subjectivity while, part **two** will be more concretized in putting the various arguments into comprehensive readable format backed-up by various contesting and appreciable case law. Both past and current cases will be enshrined into legal argument in order to, present a well balanced and appreciable juridical outcome.

It is my expectation that, this book will not only provide academic materials requisite to the study of **criminal law** but also that which will, tend to amplify hidden 'Gray areas' of the law in the application of justice. It is a common belief that criminality is an indignant and abhorrent behaviour which, society reject on the basis of stringent punishment yet, on the note of objectivism criminal mind set culminating to criminal behaviour could be considered as 'necessary evil' in the sense that, it creates a balance society for job prospect for state apprentices and at the same token, establishing the ethos of variant shift in human perspectives as mere way of life.

The impetuousness of the human world makes all the difference to that of the" world beyond" because it is not possible to simply establish "**paradise**" in our sinful world. Finally, it is my desire to extend the best of academic successes to those who may endeavour to read this book for the purpose of exams and other related professional areas within the ambit of the law.

DEDICATION

This book is dedicated to the late Hon C. A. Kamara -Taylor Second Vice- President of Sierra Leone; A.P.C. 1978 -1985 a philanthropist who, laid the foundation of my aspirations in life and gave me the deterministic courage to becoming the person, designated by destiny to be This dedication also extends to Melrose Mator Ngobeh whose moral and financial contributions enhances the completion of this book project and all former students in London, United Kingdom especially in New Harm College Stratford upon Avon, South East London College, South London Metropolitan College, West Minster College and Cambridge College to name but few where my tutorage had been of mutual benefits to enhancing, some of their university pursuit with distinctive outcome.

CHAPTER ONE

Definition of Criminal Law

Most texts on this subject, does not approach definitional style of presentation but rather, propounded on historical aspects of criminality which nevertheless, built awareness of the evolution of the subject but which unfortunately creates gaps in scholarly understanding and that of historical perspective. In order words, most students will or could be easily frustrated as they began to peruse historical passages of what constitute criminal law rather than just knowing what criminal law is within the context of any given constitution. It is my opinion that, students of law and other professionals would appreciate the fact of knowing what the subject matter is rather than, spending tireless time reading historical events after event and so on. What is essential is to let simplicity of understanding the subject be achieved through the notion of definition rather than embarking on historical journey of criminal law that tend to blur interest in the subject.

Although many definitions have been put forward as to what criminal law is by various authors yet, all of those various definitional approaches hinges on regulation of conduct of behaviour. In this respect, criminal law could now be simply and digestibly be defined as, a system or body of rules and statutes that regulates conduct of human behaviour that are prohibited by government which tend to threatens or harm public safety and welfare. Provisions are also put in place to making sure that those who tend to violate statutory code of conduct and behaviour are by and large, deemed to be exposed to the full penalties of the law by forfeiture of right of movement, association, assembly and speech especially where such offence grievously undercut peace and stability of the state in an attempt to create panic situation tantamount to ruthlessness and disaster. In most common cases, imprisonment for the aforesaid offender is common place unlike civil law which, tend to mitigate resolution of conflict between two or more people relating to property, money and damages. In short, it should be noted that, while criminal law and jurisdiction involve the state and individual; civil litigation is related to conflict resolution between individual mostly relating to property appropriation, damages with requisite fines without necessarily resulting to, restriction of fundamental human right of movement, association, assembly and speech.

Due to the nature of criminal law, the police and other law enforcement agencies or bodies, such as the secret service of the state are all involve in the pursuit to bringing offenders to accountability for the security and stability of the state. For example, a person who commits murder and disappeared become the responsibility of the state to launch a national wide search in the bid, to immediately apprehending such individual who will be termed as 'dangerous' to public safety.

What students must know is that, although, criminal offence is not committed per se against the state in real terms but rather against an individual as expostulated above, yet the state has to be involved as its' constitutional obligations to defending the fundamental human rights of its' citizens and people. In this regard, any attempt which may directly or indirectly threatened such oaths of office will be the concern of the state in dealing with the situation as a check to future occurrences. In most countries, criminality is taken to be very serious offence and therefore, is met with stringent and brutal enforcement of the law usually with Capital punishment without any reversal. Countries such as, the United States of America, Asia, The Kingdom of Saudi Arabia, and most Arab world with some third world countries to name but few, do implement penalty of such nature. In the United Kingdom during the 15TH and 16Th century, Capital punishment was very severe for even the most insignificant offences. A full historical account of punishment in England during the Elizabethan epoch will be looked at, during the course of this presentation at another chapter of this book.

In the bid to creating, a well balanced and reasonably working human society with some degree of respect for life and property, the state has to ensure that certain restrictions based on checks and balances are put in place, so that safety becomes paramount above individual interest. Criminality is ``a social taboo`` and those who find solace in such act, will face the full force of the law irrespective of status or social positions. It is against this backdrop that, the principles of democratic apparatus are entrenched within the codification of the Rule of Law. Whatsoever, the law dictates in dealing with criminal behaviour is for the common good of society in which, such dictates are made as leverages for the dignity of people and property that constitute a just society.

CHAPTER TWO

Principle of Criminal Law

Every field of study, has certain structural building blocks that laid foundation of concretized understanding of what is about to be studied or perused for quick and easy recapitulation. Criminal law is thus, no exception to this to which it is essential for students of law, to be aware of. In short, if criminal law is to be fully understood, it has to be against two possible factors without which, effort will be a mere fruitless endeavours circumvented with pinching frustration and spank. In this regard, a focus is place on **mens rea** and **actus reus.**

What is meant in criminal law by **mens rea:** Basically speaking, when we talk about the above reference, it simply means, the mental state of the individual before the aforesaid offence was committed. When a crime of murder is committed for example, that led to the apprehension of the accused person, what has to be established before the court, was the question of the accused person's state of mind when the act was committed. In order words, a question could be raised as to what the accused was thinking of before carrying out his mission. What the prosecution has to establish before a constituted court of record; was whether, the accused person's state of mind was as guilty as the act committed. If the guilty mind is established beyond all reasonable doubt as being, in concert with the act committed then the prosecution can secure a conviction against the aforesaid offender. What should be noted is that, the idea of **mens rea** varies from country to country for instance, while in most countries it is constitutionally entrenched in others, it is usually come about by precedent. Also it must be noted that, whenever, **mens rea** is required, the prosecution must prove that, the accused person's intension to bring about a particular consequence, was simultaneously in line with **actu reus**. What the accused person can safely do in defence of charges brought against him in such given circumstances is not to plead ignorance of the law but could be allowed absence of **mens rea** as an acceptable line of defence subject to verification. In order words, the accused should be allowed defence on the bases of duress in which it could be argued that, in normal mental capacity, the act of the accused could have been different. If this is the scenario, then it could be further argued that, an offender's act does not necessarily constitute a crime until a guilty mind is proven to be connected; "**actus reus non facit reum nisi mens sit rea**". It is against this background that, one tends to seemingly understand the Mental Health Act of 1983. Under this Act, it is established that, those who suffers by medical description as mentally disabled or mentally incapacitated, are hospitalised either for treatment or assessment both for public safety and for the establishment of justice. Application for assessment has to be made by an offender's nearest relative or by a qualified social worker approved by a medical doctor that the aforesaid offender was suffering from mental illness or incapacitation at the time of the offence.

Although it is commonly said that, a prosecution can only be able to secure conviction against an aforesaid offender(s), yet it is not in all situations because certain offences are classified as **strict liability** which is usually designed or implemented for business protection and that of public health and safety. In this regard, the prosecution do not necessarily have to prove the offender's mental state before conviction can be secured especially in a situation where, speed driving and the purchase of stolen goods happened to be the case. Those who are caught driving without insurance or license can't apply the test of **mens rea** as an excused to evade punishment. Seemingly, those who purchased stolen goods cannot also be opportune to rely on the mental state test especially where, the seller of such goods looks suspicious in terms of physical appearance and the location where the transaction occurred. The law has to protect genuine businesses so as to avoid economic disaster. In the interest of public safety, it is the responsibility of the state to making sure that those who commit driving offences through recklessness and negligence are brought forward for immediate punishment as a deterrent so that maximum safety on the road can be achieved. In most law books on criminal law, a mentioned of true crime and regulatory crime are emphasized to virtually mean the same as per above discussion. In order words, true crime virtually required the application of **mens** rea by the prosecution to secure conviction for the aforesaid offender(s). See **sweet v parsley** (1970). In this case it was held by the trial judge that the prosecution service needs **mens** rea in the bid to secure a conviction. On the contrary, a regulatory crime do not required the prosecution to establish intent or an intent test application to secure a conviction as already discussed in this chapter. See **Alphacell v Woodward** (1972) and **Callow v Tillstone** (1900). In these cases it was held by the judge that, selling unfit meat for public consumption and the idea of unnecessarily creating pollution which is, an environmental debacle raises no delay in the implementation of conviction as, a safe guard for public health and safety.

Footnote: Since most materials on case law are spread all over text books and other reading materials, this section of the book is designed to help gathered some of the important case law for quick referencing with synoptic summary of important area of judgement as being deliberated upon by the court at that material time. It is however essential for students, to make further research on any of the cases that will be discussed in the footnote. Starting with some of the recent case law on mens rea and actus reus will to some extent provide a better understanding of the trends of criminal adjudication as it is being expostulated by the court. In all of the cases, only key areas will be focused as guide to further reading on matters of relevance. In order words, all the cases will be presented in synoptic paraphrase so as to enable easy reading and recapitulation.

Dotterweich v. United States (Environmental Law)

It is not always true to say that, both Actus Reus and Mens Rea has to be present for a guilty verdict to be established. In most cases, where public interest and safety are at risk, whether the action of the person had no correlation of causing harm; will still be liable for his or her action. As adumbrated in the above case in which it was held that, the accused was guilty of some serious environmental disaster (2008)

Dean v. United States (2008)

Dean enters a bank, rubbing took place. He grabbed a handful of money with one hand and a loaded gun on another. Unfortunately, gun fired. Dean was accused of possessing a firearm with intent to kill. Dean argued that, since there was a total absence of intent to kill (Mens Rea), especially where no person was killed he pleaded against the submission by the prosecution to which the court however upheld that, Dean was morally involved and guilty of blameworthy act to which he was sentenced. The court further argued that, any act which is being lawfully carried out that subsequently ends in what it terms accidental mischief, the party so involved in such act, stands completely guilty of aforesaid offence.(see black stone treatment of liability under felony murder rule).

Flores- Figueroa v. United States (2009)

Accused was charged with aggravated identity theft by knowingly possessing another person's identity without his or her permission or lawful authorization. Accused pleaded not guilty on ground of innocence of not being aware of deprivation of lawful ownership of aforesaid identity. Court however upheld that, ignorance of the law is not a permissible defence against prosecution and therefore was guilty as charged within the culpability of blameworthiness.

Also see the following cases

1. Rosemand v. United States (2013)
2. Loughrin v. United States (2014)

3. Elonis v. United States (2015)

Macfadden v. United States (2015)

Footnote: It is also essential to look at some latent cases on the question of Guilty Act (actus reus) and that of the Guilty Mind (mens rea).in all of the cases, a similar trend of argument can be identified in the adjudication of verdict by the court. What should be noted however is, although it is a general rule for the prosecution to prove simultaneously both actus reus and mens rea in order to secure a convicting verdict yet, it is not always the case especially in circumstances which relates to, failure of omission. By this it means, the inability to act in preventing an offence where it is essential by virtue of connection to the aforesaid victim who relied on your protection and safety. For example, if a disabled person is in your care, it is required by law to making sure that maximum safety is guaranteed by the carer while acting in such capacity under duty of care. Failure to act in protecting the aforesaid against an assailant, constitute, negligence lack of duty of care within the parameters of common law. Although in torts law, it is not legally binding on individual to act in prevent crime or certain offences yet where it is clearly stipulated under common law that such liability exist then it becomes, tenable under duty of care for such liability to be carried out to prevent harm to others. Another example of this scenario is an occupier's responsibility to making sure that visitors' are protected against harm while in his or her premises.

Similarly, it is the responsibility of parents and guardians to protect their children against harm. For example if a toddler falls into a ditch in the presence of his /her parent liability is immediately imposed upon such parent to act in preventing harm to the child. Failure to act, constitute an offence of negligence and lack of duty of care.

Some of these cases are indeed essential to peruse for the understanding and application of criminal jurisdiction. The level of interpretation on the question of, mens rea and actus reaus can be viewed within legal rational and objectivism as expostulated in the following cases:

1. Jakeman, R V CA (1982) In this case, in which the accused was referred to as D, it was stated that, she had travelled with two suitcases of cannabis from Ghana to the UK via France where she deliberately left the suitcases in Paris. When the French Immigration and Customs Officials discovered those suitcases, the French authorities felt that, it is misrouted and thus sent it to England. On the flight, D openly repented to another traveller about the suitcases which she said, was deliberately abandoned in Paris. The question of law, relates to the issue as to whether, D was guilty of any criminal offence. It was held that, D was guilty of the aforesaid offence because, her mind set and action all constitute criminal offence.

2. Kaitamaki V The Queen (1984) PC (New Zealand), In this case, the defendant is referred to as D who was accused of rape on the following legal expostulation as thus; he entered into a young woman's flat twice and raped her. On the first encounter, penetration was not resisted and D concluded that consent is being granted and that, she was enjoying the intercourse. On the second occasion, penetration was resisted but nevertheless, D continued with the penetration until the entire exercise was finished.

Held: Guilty on the basis of restriction on second occasion while penetration was in motion.

3. Le Brun, R V (1991) CA: In this case, the defendant hit his wife unconscious and then dragged her body which made her skull to be fractured due to impact against a kerb and then later died.

Held: Although his initial action was never a precipitating factor to have culminated her death because, his mens rea could not have been tuned to killing her due to lack of such intention yet, his actus reus was sufficient to be considered as a continuation of his initial act and therefore constitute a guilty verdict of manslaughter.

4. Masilela, S V (1968). It is established in this case that, D who had an intention to knock P unconscious succeeded in doing just that, and when his victim was in this state, he set fire on the house and as a result P died due to the inhalation of toxic fume.

Held: It was held that, D was guilty because, if he had not hit him unconscious, P would have escaped from the fire equally, if the fire was caused by a tramp, a break in the causation would have occurred which could have taken the case to a new dimension in which D couldn't have been exposed to a guilty verdict.

In all these cases, it is established that, Both the mind set prior to the act (mens rea), and physical application (actus reus), has to be present for a criminal offence to take place. In extreme situation, both the mind set and the physical application can be on the verged of coincidence to secure a guilty verdict as proven in the above case scenarios.

NOTE: Where a person is in the position to prevent a disaster but simply walked away, such a person could be guilty of the outcome of whatsoever was to come. In this scenario, the question of intent is subsided in favour of will to act.

Case: A reckless person was sleeping on a mattress when he suddenly woke up and saw smoke coming from the mattress due to the cigarette he was smoking. He left the room and went into another room and fire engulfed the property.

Held: he was guilty not for causing the fire but, rather his inability to prevent the fire which, led to the inferno (Lord Diplock)

CHAPTER THREE

Pattern and Structure of Criminal Offences

In this chapter, an objective examination will be made, with regard the penal justice system obtainable and practiced during pre-industrial time in England and Wales especially during the reigned of James1 in 1603, which on several presentations by legal historians had either been over emphasised or grossly oversimplified in other to bedevilled the pre-modern penal justice system as a period of ``Bloody Code``. In order words, the pattern and structure of the justice system between 1500- 1800, was not as perpetually as brutal as being presented by some legal historians even though, some elements of capital punishment relating to hanging was common place. In this chapter, a closer examination of the various penal punishments which was prevalent at that time could be analysed as thus:

1. Capital punishment
2. Corporal punishment
3. Shipment of convicts to colonial territories
4. Fines
5. Public humiliation

In concluding this chapter, students could be able to argued as to whether, the period between1500-1800 was compounded with fair justice and biases as a bench-mark to establishing the ``logic of punishment``.

(a) CAPITAL PUNISHMENT:

This is a term in jurisdiction that is most frightening because of it horrific nature and usually barbaric way in which, it was carried out or executed on accused persons' who were found guilty of offences that relates or warrants, the application of such punishment. Between the periods of 1500-1800, in England an upsurge in convicted related crimes was recorded which led many to the gallows. The courts system at that time was more geared towards, the implementation of such punishment as mere deterrent to protect society against criminality and social disorder. It is therefore not a surprise to note that as crime rose, the courts were mandated to pronounced capital punishment even for the slightest offences such as, horse stealing, theft from churches, robbery, burglary, rape, murder, witchcraft, theft from ships either on the high sea, river or from a wharf, arson, stealing of a property that was valued one shilling, damages to public buildings and arson. What seems to be more interesting during this period was the manner in which, law makers and jurisdictional professionals were able to quickly adjust punishment pattern in accordance with social trend. For example when England went to war around 1755, employment by inscription into the King's army, saw lots of the unemployed who would have been potential criminals, were off the streets to fight in the name of queen and country.

In this regard, the level of capital punishment was substantially reduced between 1750 to1758 to an average level of, 5.6 per cent to 1.3 percent. According to J.M Beattie reference to the study of crime in southwark, a substantial number of capital related offences were reduced to pardonable level by judges. Also what most historians have excluded in their analogy was the establishment of the Ecclesiastical courts that serves as checks and balances between common law and equity. In other words, the clerical courts which were, purposely established to deal with dispute between king and church was to provide alternative forms of punishments for certain offenders which, became known as, Benefit of clergy.

Under the ecclesiastical courts, certain crimes which were deemed, to have capital punishment, were pardonable under such system as what became known as Benefit of clergy in which, accused persons were meant to confess their sins and vowed to denounce all forms of amoral behaviour and criminality.

How does benefit of clergy works? Well it is functional in the following ways; if for example an accused person is to benefit from this court, then he/she has to prove literacy of the bible by being capable of reading Psalm 51 followed by certain part of his body marked with letters such as M (representing murderer and T (representing theft as ascribed on his thumb) when all of these things are put in place, the accused person will then be set free instead of facing death by hanging.

If at any time such pardoned person comes before the clerical court with similar offences then, they will be stripped off their pardonable benefit and handed over to the lay-court to be dealt with according to law which will or culminates into the implementation of capital punishment.

(b) CORPORAL PUNISHMENT:

Between the epoch of the 16TH and 17^{Th} centuries which could be focused during the Great French Revolution and that of the reigned of the Tudors, the courts finds it more appropriate to punish convicted criminals especially those who commits minor larceny such as, theft of goods of an insignificant amount to public whipping until, the indicted person's body becomes bloody. It has to be noted that, towards the 18^{Th} century, the courts in England and Whales became subterfuge in sentencing indicted persons' of grand larceny offences to petty larceny in order to obtain public whipping. This was indeed, the beginning of capital punishment's eradication from the English legal system. In fact one would say that, the abolition of capital punishment stem out of or rather carved out of, corporal punishment. An example of corporal punishment in action, was that of a lady, who stole a chicken/ duck from a market place that worth just a shilling and was sentenced to be whipped at the full market day until her body became bloody. **(See Serah Blanley of Shrewbury's case 1721).** Although there wasn't any specific number of strokes that the courts gave yet, it could be understood that, discretion was the case in the whipping saga.

(c) SHIPMENT OF CONVICT TO COLONIAL TERRITORIES:

The over populated nature of the English prisons in conjunction with the desire to gradually put an end to the death penalty, could have been the silent factor, that motivated Humanists and the more vociferous exponents against penal system to legislatively, forced the English judiciary system to put in place certain legal mechanisms through which, capital punishment could be minimised and gradually dwindled into history. It is being suggested by some legal historians that, it isn't so much about the prevalent force or pressure of the Humanists on the government that brought about such gradual changed in the penal system but rather, the urged by the British government to develop and structurally maintained their overseas territories through man power. In other words, Britain was under the obligation to win the race of colonial territorial development against the French and as a result was gingered up to pass the 1718 act which opened the way for a more vibrant transformation of the penal system thus leading to the transportation of many convicted prisoners. What has to be noted is that, all those who had the benefit of clergy, irrespective of the nature of the offence were shipped to either the West Indies, Australia, Latin America and certain parts of Main land America as slave labourers for a duration of 6 years and subsequently

15 or more years for those who had never been cover by benefit of clergy. In short, those who have been found guilty of grand larceny such as murder, rape, serious bodily harm, arson and aggravated assaults were said to have been considered more favourably under the 1718 act simply due to been covered by benefit of clergy with lesser punishment of transportation which will be due for royal pardon after 6 years than those who commits petty larceny such as theft of a duck in a market place, subject to public flogging in the presence of friends and neighbours. Irrespective of whatsoever, history had viewed this system of punishment yet, it was indeed the foundation of the end of capital punishment in Britain.

(d) FINES:

It is not all cases either criminal or civil litigation that carries preponderant penalties as already discussed above because, some cases according to J.A Sharpe in his analysis of cases especially those that were brought for hearing at the Essex assizes between 1630 to 1700, were exposed to settlement by fining of about few pence to few shillings. Fines were of two folds; fixed and variable which were simultaneously levelled by the judiciary. Under the reign of James1 a fixed penalty fine was levelled against all drunkards who became public nuisance and seemingly a spectacle of embarrassment to both king and country.

The level of fines varied between the ordinary working persons and those of high social affluent. For example, those working class whose wages were minimal, were usually exposed to low or small fines for minor offences such as; frauds, common assaults, battery and other petty related issues such as the flouting of official regulations. It was reported that, when Duke of Devonshire William assaulted a man within the environs of the king's palace, a fine of £30,000 was levelled against him that indicated that fines were levelled according to status and class.

Usually, the courts could decide to allow both the defendant and the prosecutor to come up with agreeable pattern of settlement however if on the contrary, this is not achieved then, the court will impose its' own level of fines that could be or may be stressful. Since the epoch of the 16th century fines have been part of the English legal penal system to date.

(e) PUBLIC HUMILIATION:

The church and the state have concurrent patterns of dealing with offenders especially during the epoch of 1500 in England. Still on the question of avoiding capital punishment for offenders, the courts were able to devised a method of punishing offenders or those whose behaviour tend to deviate, from the acceptable norms of society so that, sanity and cordiality of behaviour could be maintained and sustained as moral ethos for decency of society. The Pillory System was thus invented and firmly put in place, to dealing with offences relating to homosexuality, child molestation, cheating, selling of defective goods or goods not fit for purpose or as described, uttering of seditious words or writing negative and unfounded story about people, engaged in act of adultery and fornication, stealing and those found in act of indecency and unclean behaviour especially with children.

These punishments were administered by the secular courts in conjunction with the judiciary for efficacy. The methods involved in applying the pillory system of punishment varied in many aspects depending on the nature and scope of the offence. Basically, it was designed to shame publicly those found guilty of acts contrary to the acceptable norms of the English society at that material time. In the secular domain, a person that is found guilty of act of cheating, could be made to stand in front of the congregation during full Sunday service with head bowed and a piece of paper round his or her neck depicting the offence committed. Other forms of pillorying relates to offenders being put on a wooding device and made to stand on full market day with an inscription of the offence boldly, written on his or her chest for all to see. Others could be placed on a public bench with both legs clamped and an inscription depicting the offence committed in bold letters on his or her chest for all to see for hours. For example in 1751,a woman who stole a piece of cloth from St' Saviour's Parish, was made to stand in the workhouse vicinity once a week while in the same token, in Wandsworth, a woman was made to stand on a stool for an hour in public. It should be note that, all of these forms of penal punishments were designed as means of preparing the way for the eradication of capital punishment which was, becoming too frequent and in most cases found to be inhumane and unjustifiable.

CHAPTER FOUR

(F) Class Related Criminal Behaviour And The Leverage Of Punishment:

Is there any such thing as, ``class criminal related behaviour`` or is there any rational suggestion to support the argument that, certain class of people are prone naturally to specific crime and that nothing whatsoever, could be done to remedy such awful patterns of behaviour. Basically speaking, it couldn't be surprising to note that, when social structure is patterned along such negative ideology certain class of people could be affected unjustifiably irrespective of establishment of innocence. The question is, why should certain class of people considered as prone to specific crime and others are not? In order words, does guilt goes before the establishment of innocence in adjudication?

It is a common practice in law that, an accused person(s), are deemed to be innocent in the phase of the law until, being legally tried and found guilty in a legally constituted court of the land before, sentencing can be made effective. Any deviation from such serenity of law, leads to constitutional breach and thus, becomes questionable in the interpretation of fair justice within the ambits of a truly democratic society. It is therefore found wanting to note that, while certain report tend to tilt the scale of fair reporting on crime due to class differences and patterns of social structure, the true reality of fair play remain untouched in most cases for the satisfaction of the upper class in their dominance of the social structure.

It is without doubt that, the idea of class related crime is a social construct which is aimed at creating class distinctions between the haves and the have not. Over the years, ethnic minority in the western hemisphere especially in the United Kingdom, Germany, United States of America to name but few, have had a vibrant struggle with this scenario of specific crime relating to specific ethnic migrants such as; those of Afro-African descent whose criminality for survival in the area of gun crime, theft, fraud against business, vehicle- related theft and burglary, violent against a person(s) and above all, drugs- related arson, rape and murder. During the epoch of the Brixton Riot in the 1980s, which triggered the Scarman's report on the causes and it effects had on the social patterns of the British society; it was discovered that, the black youths were exposed to police targeted crime surveillance as against their white counterparts. During this dark period, black youths were targeted as prone to high level of criminalities in all aspects of life without, taken into consideration the back ground that provoked such social malaise.

Lord Scarman's report thus high-lighted the fact that, until and unless certain structures are put in place, to revamp structural adjustment in dealing with youth unemployment, education, housing, social amenities and better police training in creating mutual understanding and trust within the community the serve, worst incident of an unimaginable scale will engulf Britain, strangulating race relationship. Following the publication of this report, so many things that were not in place became the focus and primary concern of government in an attempt to creating a balanced society where the Rule of Law, operates fairly without prejudice and social exclusion. After this report, it became evident that police recorded crime though could not be excluded in its' totality because it gives us certain information about day-to-day criminal activities yet, could not be relied upon for any statistical evidence where compilation of recorded crime between England and Wales are concern (see CSEW-crime survey for England and Wales 2017).

It is now been established with reasonable ease that, there is no class that is specifically known or could be linked to specific crime-related behaviour other than being a ``social construct'' in which certain class of people are termed as ``devils'' and others as angelic. In the United States of America, Afro Americans are more likely to be arrested and sent to prison for even minor offences such as minor traffic violation of parking on the wrong side of the road. In most cases, police have planted fake evidence in the vehicles of Afro Americans in order to prove and justify their arrest for prosecution that ends in an unjustifiable imprisonment of their victims.

It is against this backdrop that miscarriage of justice is identified and expunged. What mostly constitute criminal behaviour could be within the leveraged of social explanation as to why the less privileged and economically downtrodden are by virtual of circumstances beyond control, engaged in petty crime for survival. Today in all the prisons around the world, in mates are more reflective of lower or economical disadvantage class than those from high- profile status. In order words, there are more prisoners emanating from the economic class as compared to those from the upper class. If one may be tempted to raise issue concerning this sort of trend, economic and social factors could not be avoided because it is true this that, proper and requisite understanding as to how fair, the justice system operates in our society. It is easier for those who fall below the political and socio-economic advantage of life to be, treated with harshness of the law than those who, because of their high profile status. For instance, in England during the epoch of the 17th century a highly educated solicitor's son was charged for issuing false shares certificates to customers but unfortunately never brought to court to face the reality of his crime rather, he continued issuing fake certificates to his victims till 1930 when he was finally apprehended and the case disappeared under the ``carpet''. If William Preston had been a poor person, his son would have been given the longest jail sentence but instead, his son was able to outlast the justice system that brought sentences of forgery against him since 1894, 1902 and 1910. In contrast to this, in 1578, a gentleman by the name of John Bellman, of St John Street in Clerkenwell was paraded in a cart in the presence of neighbours for illegally dealing with a woman he wasn't supposed to. Seemingly, heavy punishment was mitted out to a woman due to share poverty who, stole a piece of chicken and was exposed to public humiliation by standing on a public bench in Wandsworth with the evidence of theft in her hands for all to see for a duration of time specified by the authority.

It was not surprising therefore to note that, the invention of so called "White-Collar Crime" was an undemocratic ideology which tend to give special treatments to some people because of their high social profile as against the rest of society under which the true spirit of human confidence in the 'self' is inundated with fear and malicious suspicion.

Those who may succumb to such, evaporate themselves as It preaches the "gospel" of segregation, nepotism, racial ethnic divide, regionalism and nationalism. Under such maxim, the poor and the socially marginalised are relegated to the back drop of society where their voices are only herd by mysticism of creation for mercy and fair justice. No wander a reputable writer of law, Canon Horsley said in his book entitled, (**Haw criminals are made and prevented 1913**), pointed out that, statically evidence of the percentage of crime of White- Collar, could not be accessed either for lack of police recording or such cases never got through the judicial process of prosecution but rather were settled at civil spectrum. In order words, such crime most often, where dismissed as mere slander or propagation against persons of higher social calibre.

The issue of fair justice for 'all' could it be a mere myth or a play on words by those whose technicality of language, tend to muddle factuality with double standard behaviour. Should certain category or class of people be accorded with, favourable treatment before the phase of the law while others are meant to, languish behind bars simply because of their class position? It is without doubt that, justice should be mitted out to all on the basis of fairness without any militating issue relating to class position and that those who are found, in violation of this fundamental principle of natural justice, should and must be exposed to the full penalty of the law. In this regard, people who due to special reasons may tend to wobble and trifled with justice, should be identified and exposed to stringent judicial measures as defined within the constitution of the aforesaid land.

A fair judicial system must be put in place with, relative degree of functional independence from the rest of the organs of government so that, interpretation of the law, can be without fear of political reprisals. Those who are given the task of administrating the law must be, competently qualified with bias-free mentality in the deliberation of justice within the ambit of the **Rule of Law.**

CHAPTER FIVE

The Structure of law enforcement and Rule of Law

This chapter looks at procedures which are required, for cases to be brought to court for hiring or deliberations. It should be noted that, legal proceedings are not necessarily the same as it differs from one territory to another with specific reference to system of government, religious and cultural practice. For example, under a Unitary or cabinet system of government which are sometimes referred to as, Parliamentary system practiced in the United Kingdom, the structure of law enforcement are basically examined within Criminal and Civil Litigation. All matters of criminal nature such as rape, murder, theft, assaults, accident and traffic offences, arsons, burglary, treasons, libel and sedition to name but few, are channelled through the police, crown prosecution service which initially investigate matters relating to the above before if any, former charges could be brought against an accused person(s) or an establishment within the frame work of the rule of law. Seemingly, all matters relating to civil litigations, is that which usually occurs between two individuals relating to debt payment, property appropriation, dispute, repossession, eviction, marriage and divorcement that is channelled directly to court by the parties involved either through their legal representatives or themselves without, the involvement of the police and the crown prosecution service (CPS).

In a Federal system, complexity in the enforcement of law is absolutely glaring because of, differences in States to States legislations that interprets the law within their legal jurisdictions. In other words, what is considered in one State as major offence other States could considered such as minor. Furtherance to this, what is considered as chargeable offence in one State, could be allowed as a way of life in another. In Los Angeles for instance, Gay and Lesbian marriage is allowed as a way of life while in certain States especially in Philadelphia, is considered as both immoral and unconstitutional

Irrespective of Geo-regional differences in the enforcement of law yet, certain facts are usually placed in common for the prevalent of equal justice and fair play. If unfortunately, this is not put in place and diligently observed and practiced, the protection of people and society will be fragile culminating into, chaos and massacre in which fundamental human rights will be obscured and debunked into history books.

The police which is an instrument of State controlled mechanism, or State apparatus, being charged with the responsibility of protecting society and people against acts that tend to, create civil disobedience and violence through its' length and width policing patrols as enshrined in the constitution of any given country; can be more effective if, an effective establishment of the Rule of law and unbiased constituted court system are in entrenched in the constitution. It is therefore the more reason why, every democratic country are expected to have an established constituted judicial system based upon the principles of the rule of law for the implementation of, free and fair equitable justice for all irrespective of ethnicity, religion, sectionalism, political affiliation and race. What has to be noted is that, although the police have the power of arrest and detained suspects in connection with, criminal behaviour or activities yet, it has to be within the confined of the rule of law as enshrined in the constitution of the aforesaid country. At this junction, it is essential to examine what is meant by Rule of Law and why it is a cogent constitutional bed-rock of democracy.

(a) Rule of Law: according to a British professor while looking and accessing the efficacy of the British constitution, he was able to state clearly in 1885 that, supremacy of the law must override common interest and equally above party politics and vested social interest. Law he went on to argued, must remain superior and that superiority must be respected and maintained at all cost. Parliament which makes the law, must at all times, remain superior and strictly subservient to the core values of what it has established either in codification or none codification. Professor Dicey also stated that, under the principles of the rule of law, equality before the law is paramount irrespective of one's status in society and that every one irrespective of the nature of the crime committed, are first deemed innocent until later proven by a legally constituted court, to be guilty before sentencing can be effective against the aforesaid accused person(s). In this regard, let us now examined some of the criteria which constitute effective mechanism of the rule of law as expostulated by one British legal expert as thus:

(b) Legal Certainty. This is the most important area which has to be guided and effectively implemented at all times if respectability for the law is to be achieved. In this regard, any law which is passed must be effectively carried out and enforced without which it becomes a mere spectacle of mockery and oblivion.

(c) Equality. Equal treatment before the phase of the law is another cogent area which makes the constitution of any country respectable, firmly established, easily workable for the maintenance of order and for the creation of international recognition. Equality in simple terms means that, all shall be treated with respect before the phase of the law irrespective of race, colour, origin, tribal and territorial demarcations, political affiliations, social connections and positions. In this regard, the law must treat all accused persons innocent until later proven guilty in a legally constituted court of the law of superior record before, judgement can be implemented. It is under this notion that the concept of **habeas corpus** which is a prerogative writ used to challenge the legality of one's detention issued mostly by provisional court of the Queen's Bench division in the United Kingdom in retrospect of the application of fair justice.

(d) Fairness. All written laws have to be clearly readable or legible to ensure clarity and to prevent discrimination in it implementation and interpretation. Any law which is written in ``crab text,`` allows minimal readability and comprehension and thus, negate the fundamental ethos of fair play and retributive justice. Since most of the laws are written in technical or legal terms therefore, those who are professionals must endeavour to interpret it simplistically to those who none legal. This is the reason why judges and magistrates including other legally interpretative bodies, are required to say what the law is and why it is applicably interpreted in the manner in which, it is been interpreted.

(e) Retrogressive laws. This is very hostile in the phase of democratic society that believes in the dignity of human rights because it tend to stifle it's application by identifying persons who had not been, convicted of an offence at the time it was said to have been committed due to, it none criminal nature but can now be prosecuted for sentencing. In a nutshell, offences that have been none criminal for which accused persons have not been jailed for could now be reopened for trial for possible sentencing.

(f) Due process. This clearly depicts the way in which courts and other legally recognised institution like the police handled reported incident criminal related matters or offences. In this regard, all accused persons has to be tried by a legally constituted courts and if found guilty, punished in accordance with the law. Unnecessary delay in trials, by and large constitute denial of justice and fair play. Under this criteria those who might have been unlawfully imprisoned without trial, are entitled to compensation for damages as dictated by law. In nutshell, no person should be kept in custody over and above what the constitution stipulate. In addition to this, no person should be arrested without warrant or without being told what offences they have committed. The suspect has the right to remain silent and must not be forced to say or make statements without legal representation. If in most cases depending on which country it is applied, a person is not charged within specific time frame as dictated by the constitution of the aforesaid country, then immediate release of the suspect most take effect.

NOTE: **in 1765 a case in the UK established the principle of the rule of law with reference to Entick v Carrington.** In this case, it was established that those who carry out the law must have the legal authority of doing so or else, will be tantamount to illegality and thus unacceptable. In paraphrase, it was stated in this case that, a police officer entered Entick resident and seized property followed by his arrest without warrant. The court was quick to find the police officer guilty of illegal entry and arrest of Entick and the police was made to pay for damages and loss of property.

CHAPTER SIX

Various levels and interpretation of criminal law

Interpretation of criminal law as of all other law cases is that of the court, to deliberate on the application as presented before it, for jurisdiction within the whims of its competence where necessary or otherwise, being referred to another courts of superior record as stipulated in the constitution of the aforesaid land. There are various levels of criminal interpretation of which some are minor and others are major. Some of the offences are indictable and others are none depending on the nature and gravity of the offence. In this chapter, act which constitute both minor and major criminal offences will be listed and synoptically discussed so that, distinctive clarity can be made, to avoid duplicity and wobbling where matters of such nature are to be referred to. In this regard hitherto, the following are reasonably essential to be noted under criminal type of offences as thus:

1. Murder (homicide, lawful and unlawful)
2. Manslaughter(voluntary and involuntary)
3. Assault(battery- intentional/reckless application of force to a person without consent)
4. Property Crime (burglary, arson)

5. Larceny (theft and rubbery)
6. Fraud (act of obtaining something by deception)
7. Handling stolen property
8. Road traffic offences (reckless driving/drink driving)

For the purpose of clarity and simplistic understanding, it is but essential to briefly discuss each of the high-lighted subtopics, for a recapitulation exercise especially, where duplicity of facts tend be interwoven with jurisdiction.

(1)Homicide: This simply means murder as one of the most serious major criminal offences which, translate as the unlawful killing of a reasonable person under the protection of the king's peace and protection, death resulting within a year and a day **(See Coke's definition, law of England 1797)**

Basically speaking, what has to be noted is a modification in Coke's definition in which the question of, ``one year and a day``, for the qualification of murder to be considered. Modification was brought about by The Criminal Law Revision Committee Report on Offences Against the person, 1784-1980 stipulating that, it could be legally and morally wrong for an accused person to remain free without been brought for trial until a year and a month, for the justification of murder. Also due to advanced medical technology, it is now being possible to keep patient who otherwise could have died instant, to be kept under life supporting machine for as long as it takes. This means that, if Coke's definition of murder is to be applied, it could have had a negative effect on the implementation of equitable justice and fair play since an accused person, could have remained indefinite without trial. As a result of this, the house of parliament moved swiftly to enact a law to bring into effect the 1996 Act, to abolish Coke's definition of murder relating to ``one year and a month``.

In nowadays language, homicide con be deduced to manslaughter and infanticide, and to some extent child destruction in the form of abortion, depending on the existing law of the aforesaid land. This means in certain part of the world, child destruction in the form of abortion is constitutionally permissible while in certain countries is a major criminal offence punishable by death. Also, suicide is constitutionally unjustifiable and those who attempt to take their own life, shall be exposed to murder investigation and if found guilty shall be punished by law and those who may aid the killing of another person upon permission, shall be liable for prosecution for manslaughter. Seemingly, if two persons' agreed to take each other's life,(suicide pact) and one happened to survive, that person shall be equally charged for murder under manslaughter. The argument to prosecute suicidal of any description, is more of a moral issue than constitutional because, since it is the obligation of the state, to protect its' citizens and residents against criminality and any acts of aggression, therefore, it is morally wrong for one to do same.

Murder of any description can either be lawful or unlawful. What constitutes lawful murder is when a person acting in self defence or using reasonable force to prevent crime and as a result death occurs without intent. On the centrally, where intent to harm result to death, such is considered as unlawful murder.

Murder of any legal description, could either be premeditated or none as expressed within malice aforethought which can be divided into three sectors such as; **express, implied** and **constructive malice aforethought**. Reference to express malice aforethought, is the case in which an expression of hostility is present with intent to kill. In this case scenario, both mental intent and the will to act are simultaneously merged for the aforesaid purpose **(see mens rea/actus reus)**. Implied malice aforethought is the case scenario in which an act is committed with intent to inflict grievous bodily harm on the victim but unfortunately, result to death. Constructive malice aforethought is murder related offence in which, the accused act either in self defence or preventing the victim from committing felony or resisting arrest for the aforesaid offence that, culminate to the killing of the victim. For example, if a police man in the course of restraining a person from committing felony result to the death of that person, murder will be construed as constructive malice aforethought. However, it will be left with the trial judge to examine whether, excessive force could be applicable or reasonable force in the bid to restraining aforesaid victim. It will also be decided by definition of law, what constitutes **excessive force** and what could be acceptable as **reasonable force**.

(2)Manslaughter: This is considered as homicide but could not be legally constituted as murder because of various legal parameters that could be involved in which **intension** and **action** could be required as proofs for the adjudication of justice. For example, if an accused person illegally enters into his victim's premises to steal and unfortunately was met with fierce resistance in which, he shot his victim and left him bleeding resulting to his death, a guilty verdict of manslaughter could be upheld. What has to be noted is, whether the accused person did enter his victim's premises to kill or to steal. Also it will be established as to whether carrying fire arm constitutes an intension to kill under implied malice aforethought. If it is proven that implied malice aforethought is the motivating factor for such acts, **voluntary manslaughter** could be upheld. Seemingly, involuntary manslaughter verdict could be upheld if, an act result to death under the influence of alcohol or an accused person is being drunk in which the state of his mind is adversely affected in terms of seasonable thinking. If this is to be established under the **Homicide Act 1957, section 2**, then the question of **Diminished Responsibility** is to be addressed.

Footnote on some important Homicide cases in the United Kingdom

1. **R.v. Vickers (1957), this was a test case in which, appellant went to steal and upon entry the premises, he saw an elderly woman of 72 years of age on the upper floor and in the bide of hiding evidence of illegal entry and theft, attacked the victim with several struck on her head followed by multiples kicks on her side which resulted to the victim's death. It was held that, under sections 1(1) of the Homicide Acts of 1957, where a person engages in act of felony either violent or non- violent, which result to death such shall be considered as murder under constructive malice aforethought**

2. R. V. Smith (1961). The House of Lords deliberated on this case several to come up with a reputable judgement to overturn manslaughter verdict to a capital punishment of murder under the aforesaid Acts of 1957. In this case it was argued that, the suspected driver of the vehicle carrying stolen goods stopped by a police man would have foresaw that, while he was been interrogated, he was under duty obligation to comply with instruction but instead, maliciously pulled away while the police man was hanging on his car door in which, an incoming vehicle on the opposite direction slammed into the police man which killed him instantly. In this case, it was argued by the Law Lords that, the driver clearly and unambiguously foresaw that, his action was dangerous and that it could result to fatality and still continued with his reckless and dangerous behaviour which result to the death of his victim to which the verdict of murder could have been requisite

3. R. V. Hyam (1957) this was a case scenario in which the presentation of Ellenborough Act of 1803 was put to the test by Lord Diplock and Lord Kilbrondon in which they argued that, where intent to cause bodily harm is established which result to the victim's death, such will be interpreted as murder even where intent to murder at prima facia was never the issue but could have had an impact on the question of the foreseen test in which any reasonable person, could have realised that such action could produced or result to fatality and death to have been avoided.

4. R. V. Cunningham (1981). The Cunningham case is a classical example of the foreseen test scenario in which the accused argued that, he was carried by uncontrollable jealousy upon suspecting that, the lady he was to have married was having affairs with the victim. In this regard, the victim was struck severally on the head with severe blows resulting to his death. Although the accused argued that his action was not intended to cause death yet, it was overturned on the basis of his inability to realise that, his action was going to produce fatality and therefore to have refrained from such but rather, choose to continue knowing what the outcome of his behaviour was going to be.

5. R. V. Doughty. Appellant case for manslaughter was rejected by the Lords in favour of murder on the ground that, his defence of, provocation which militated his action of killing his 17 days old

child for being restless and persistently crying was understood by the Lords as negligence and lack of duty of care which, every born child needs from parents in which, he woefully have failed in his responsibility which the child deeply needed.

(3) Assault. Legally speaking, assault is considered as trespass against a person with intent to do harm to such person in variety of ways such as abduction, rape and rob. It is also being considered as any reckless act exemplified against a person(s), with intent to cause physical or psychological trauma or injury to the aforesaid victim. Assault could be intentional in which case, direct malice aforethought is applied as the more reason why, the act was carried out against the victim. It could also be reckless in nature with no intent to cause physical harm but which, could constitute verbal or common expression of anger against a person that could be distressing and thereby causing psychological trauma and sleeplessness to the aforesaid victim. For instance, a person who expresses excessive anger by waving a cutlass against another person or by verbally threatening his neighbour's peace could be guilty of common assault by definition of which if, such is in the United States of America could be constituted as **misdemeanour** which is lesser than the offence of **felony**. Here are a few samples of cases involving Assault as expostulated in judgement in the English Court of Law:

1. **Fagan v. Metropolitan Police Commissioner (1969). In this case, a police man ordered a driver to park his car on a particular spot of which he ended parking on the police man's foot and refused to reverse for couple of seconds. He was later charged for physical assault with intent to cause injury to his victim. An appeal against conviction was crushed on the basis that, assault on a person either by placing a hand on that person without permission could just constitute same as using a stick as extension of the hand to carry out the touching. Therefore sitting in a car while the tyre of the car is resting on the foot of a person without making an immediate attempt to reverse the car, will be interpreted as psychical assault to the victim as upheld by Lord Parker C.J supported by Lord Bridge J**

1. R. v. Ireland; R. V. Burstow (1997) House of Lords.

This was another case law in which assault was deliberated at length by the House of Lords in an attempt, to legally established whether, expression of words or by mere silence of intermittent calls to a victim, could constitute an offence leading to assault. In this case, the accused, Ireland was held guilty of making numerous silent calls to several women, who over those periods of time, developed and suffered psychological stress and trauma leading to sleeplessness, anxiety, mental abnormality and palpitation.

His appeal was dismissed by the House of Lords, under s.47 of the Act of 1861 which clearly specified offences against a person. In his judgement, Lord Steyn robustly disagrees with Counsel for the defence when he argued that, ``words alone do constitute assault just as silence``, in this, Lord Steyn concluded that, words which tend to trigger fear in the mind of the victim constitute assault especially where such words threatens the security of the victim. He also added that ``a thing said is a thing done``. In his final submission, he concluded that, it will be highly unthinkable to suggest that, a man who comes across a woman on a lonely footpath saying to her, ``follow me or else you die`` couldn't be considered a mere joke.

A silent caller who made menacing telephone calls to his victim saying that, he will be at her door steps in few second, will be guilty of assault under section 47, of 1861 Act (offence against the persons act). Such call leads to psychological trauma as an invasion of the victim peace of mind.

Depending on the nature of the situation as to where the offence had been committed, assault could be construed accordingly either intentionally or recklessly.

(4)Property crime (Burglary and arson) it is an established fact that, everyone is entitled to the peace and comfort of their home and as such anything that tend to disturb/ undermined such freedom will constitute, unless otherwise by legal requirement or proclamation which tend to withdraw or suspend such freedom or right as established by court order such as warrant of entry by bailiffs. In the absence of such order, any attempt otherwise will constitute a breach of privacy and comfort of property. The question is, under what circumstances property crime occurs? The simple explanation is uninvited entry with intent to steal, vandalised and even threatens life of the occupant. Under the 1968 theft Act, burglary can be expressed in terms of intent/without intent. No matter the proscription of its definition, it synonymously constitutes trespass against a person which takes the dimension of either rape or criminal damage and arson. When burglary is expressed as aggravated it means a much more serious situation in which the trespasser carries fire arms, explosives and other dangerous weapons to committee battery against a person(s). Under the 1997/1998 Acts, maximum sentence is usually life imprisonment with impunity. In synopsis, when we talk about burglary, it could simply be referred at point of reference of case law to mean the following:

1. **A trespasser who enters a building or any part of a building with intent either to steal or inflict harm on the legal occupant of the aforesaid building either intentionally or unintentionally as stipulated under the 1991Criminal Justice Act as amended under sections 26(2).**
2. **2. After haven entered with permission on the bases of invitation, infringed upon the invitation by, entering into a restricted part or area of the building with a warning sing, "RESTRICTED AREA".**
3. **3. A trespasser who wittingly uses an object to unlock the windows and at the same time, uses the object to fished out or removed the valuable items on the table because his physical hands couldn't reach out to accomplish his criminal act, shall be liable for burglary under the aforesaid Act for using abject as an extension of his physical hands.**

Ref Cases:

A. R. V. Hughes (1785)

In this case, the accused was known as H, had an intention to steal valuables from the property with the desire to permanently deprived the

owner of it but due to the nature of the door, he used an object to undo the door without his physical presence in the building. It was held that, bur glary had taken place

What was noted in this trial after H was guilty of burglary, his defence counsel, file an appeal against the conviction of his client on the following ground that; although burglarious entry of nay nature constitute an offence against the legal instrument, under the aforesaid Act, yet, where previous breakages had been the case of the property, the question of breaking could not be sufficient enough to attest the validity of burglary especially where there was no new breakage

B. R.V. Bailey (1818). Although in the case of H the accused person was acquitted from prison on technicality of terms, in the case of Bailey it was different because it was established and with held by the Law Lords that, for burglary to be illegal entry has to effective and sufficient or else, it will be an attempted burglary. SEE R.V.COLLINS, R.V.RYAN (1996).

On the question of arson, the issue of intent is always the key factor that the law considered in establishing a case for arson. Basically, when intentionally or none intentional, a person set fire on another man's property with the aim of not only to destroy the structure of the property but also to kill its' occupants then arson will be construed accordingly. Recklessness could to some extent, constitutes arson if it is established beyond reasonable doubt that, danger was unquestionably envisaged that such action could produced a catastrophic end. For example, if a man while pumping fuel in his car took a match and light his pipe to smoke of which in the process, an inferno ensued engulfing properties and lives shall be liable for arson under negligence and recklessness with intent to cause death and destruction. Seemingly if a person with mental problem, pull up his car to a petro/ fuel station to put fuel in his car, suddenly lights up his cigarette which results to an inferno should this be considered as, an act of intent based on negligence and recklessness? If it has to be established before a legally constituted body that arson did occur and that charges in lure of negligence and recklessness has to be, inseparably considered for verdict to be handed out, then the question that follows, shall be of two folds:

(a) To what extent does a mentally incapacitated person be liable for his/ her action? In other words, does action of a mentally diminished person correlates to intent. Or better still, could it be argued that, a person of such incapacitated mental dimension really and actually meant to cause death and destruction by his/ her aforesaid action. The law has to be précised in its deliberation as to whether a person of such deranged condition, could be capable of inflicting harm with intent to others. Objectively, it is without doubt that, any person has the ability to inflict harm on themselves and to others but on the question of criminal law, does intent and action with regard to a person that falls in such descriptive category, constitute any legal leverage upon which negligence and recklessness could be considered for a guilty verdict. Thus if it is complex or rather difficult to establish verdict on the basis of intent related action, a situation will arise where vicarious liability has to be an option to be considered as to who should be responsible for the action of insanity. Could it be institutional liability for haven deliberately knowingly that such person, will be prone to committing crime against himself and other innocent people and yet, allowed to socialise as if being a normal person. It is without doubt that, under such circumstances, the social services of the state, could to some extent, have some questioning as to why, restraint on such person was not adequately put in place, for the safety of society.

(b) Conversely, if a normal person enters a building as a trespasser with intent to steal and unfortunately, just at the point of leaving the building a large explosion engulfed the building. Later, the trespasser was arrested and charged for theft and arson. The question of law is whether, the accused person could be charged for theft and arson. What should be note is the establishment of intent which has to be examined as to what purpose the accused person did enter the building in the first place though as a trespasser. If it is proven that, intent to steal was the purpose then it constitutes a leverage of none arson since arson as a motive couldn't be sufficiently established. What the law should be concerned with is theft which was the established intent that was carried out preceded by action.

(c) Should a situation arise where, a person while amongst his friends watching telecast, made a remark following a news bulleting about an arson attack on a building saying; ``i am very pleased that the work is done for me``. If such a person is arrested later for arson, should there be any defence mechanism upon which his innocence or guilt could be established? It is without doubt that, remark such as this, could attract the attention of the law enforcement officers in the bid to establishing the circumstances in which such remark was made and the significant or meaning of it. In a typical case sample, in which for the purpose of legal argument the accused could be represented by `**B**` who explicitly told the magistrate that, his innocence of the arson attack is unquestionable since his involvement physical was non participatory. The crown prosecutor will then have to convince the magistrate that, physical participation was not sufficient enough for the extrication of the accused since, his wishes where accomplished on the basis of intent. It could also be argued that, those arsonists where the remote physical representation of `**B**` who might or could have hired or paid for the act and thus, such remarks. His remark made him a suspect and therefore an accomplished to the act as expostulated by the prosecution team. Carelessness or recklessness of speech and of action especially in a public domain, carries some degree of concern especially where, threat to life and property are at the periphery of destruction. Whatever the outcome of this case will or could depend on which way the argument is at best.

What has to be stated categorically is whether, the law as it stands, has any concern over issues no matters how trivial or insignificant it may appear, if it has direct or indirect effects on peoples' way of life. Under the **Rule of Law** innocent of the law could not necessary be excusable especially where pre-knowledge of the penal code is well known however, where access to the penal code is not made available to the rest of society but rather kept for the few, such could be questionable as to why. In this regard, innocence in terms of breach could be objectively argued within the context of informative obstruction and secrecy.

The principles of the Rule of Law, is a democratic apparatus which protects and defend the fundamental human rights irrespective of race, colour, creed, religion, place of origin and culture. It is on the note of this that, all accused person(s), are deemed innocent until later proven guilty. Under such note, no person shall be arrested without warrant or without been told what the offence or crime the individual had committed. Those who may or are arrested and taken to the police station for questioning, must be charged to appear before court in lure of the aforesaid offence, rather than been kept in police custody indefinitely irrespective of the gravity of the accusation.

5.Larceny (Theft and rubbery) most text books have not been able to make clear distinctions between what constitute theft and that of rubbery and as such, dubiousness of understanding prevails. In most instances, students of law, finds it difficult to establish what constitute theft from rubbery which usually create series of loop holes in the understanding and application of the law, where it is deemed necessary. It is hoped that, clarity of explanation would endeavour distinctive understanding of this area of law. Basically speaking, larceny is considered as, the most serious criminal offence. There are various classifications of larceny which is at this stage, not the concern of this topic under discussion. In this regard, a simplistic approach of what is theft is defined as, an illegal act of taking property from its legitimate owner with the intention of permanent deprivation of the aforesaid owner. If for example, a person enters a building as a trespasser or part of it, and take property without permission such constitute theft by definition. If on the other hand, a trespasser enters a building or part of a building taking properties unauthorised and while exciting the premises a huge explosion engulfed the building that left him seriously burnt. As police an ambulance attended the crime scene, he was arrested and charged for theft and arson. The question was, whether he could be charged for arson. It was stated that, since he entered the premises with the intention to steal which he was able to accomplished, arson was an incident which fell out of his intention and physical involvement. He could be charged nevertheless, for theft but not, arson. Rubbery is another kind of obtaining property illegally but with face- to-face confrontation with the legitimate owner in which, threats of violence is applied. It is usually classified under petty theft in which, owners of properties are put under duress or threat, to kill if resistance is applied. Examples of such case scenario are, snatching of mobile phones, watches, jewelleries and money. What should be noted is the gravity of the crime for example, if a person is put under gun point and his car is taken away although the establishment of the point of contact is made, such constitute a very serious criminal offence which could not be under petty theft but rather a very serious offence under larceny. **See the following cases on theft as follows: in the case of Lawrence VS MPC (1972) a student took a taxi ride and was asked to pay 50p upon arrival, the student offered a £1 note to the driver who took the money and requested additional £5.00 more. When the student refused, defendant took £5.00 from her wallet. It was held that, the driver acted illegally and that, taking the extra money without the owner's consent constitute theft. Also see R VS Morris and Aderton Vs Burside (1984) in which defendants were caught swapping prices of items to favour their purchase that was considered by Lord Roskill as an appropriation based on intent to deprive the seller/owner actual original price**

6. fraud (act of obtaining something by deception).when the term fraud is used, it should be essential to make clarification as to what constitute fraud and what by and large, is to be deemed as swindle. Basically, when fraud is mentioned it means an illegal act or behaviour in which a person obtained goods/items by deception.

Such deceptive behaviour, amount to theft. Swindle on the other hand, is where a swindler, manipulate the owner of an item so that, he becomes the owner. Such is not usually punishable under common law with the exception where, forgery of documentation is involved. In this regard, a thief and a swindler are to a great extent, one and the same. If for instance, `A` dressed up as a police officer to stop and seized unlicensed vehicle on the motorway which led to his arrest and charged for impersonation and theft. In the same token, `B` appear casual dropping leaflets in the nearby neighbourhood introducing himself as, a mechanic who can repair cars on discount basis with further incentive of ``pay only when car is repaired to satisfaction``. Unfortunately, the people he was dealing with, never knew that he was a swindler until when apprehended by the police after several reports and surveillance. The question arises as to whether `B` who is a classical swindler, could be charged for theft analogous that of `A`. Under the 1916 larceny Act section32 which deals with the issue of obtaining something by pretences could be read jointly by the forgery Act 1861, section3 and the false impersonation Act 1874, section1. From the point of common law, a swindler could not be charge for theft by deception but where impersonation or forgery of documentation is involved then the 1874 Act is immediately triggered under section 1 of the aforesaid Act. Under the Criminal Justice Act1991, 24(4) whether an item is obtained by deception or stolen, it is punishable by more than seven years imprisonment on the basis of theft. A closer examination of the theft Act 1968, section 15 clearly states that; any person who by any act of deception dishonestly obtained another person's property with the intention of permanently depriving such owner of its use, shall be guilty of theft and if found guilty shall be liable for imprisonment not exceeding ten years.

CHAPTER SEVEN

In this chapter, a brief but précised discussion will be put across explaining the philosophy of modern criminality and how, it has found expression in religion, culture, traditional values and race. In connection with this approach, a rational examination based on moral ethics and evaluations as to why criminality is on the increase in the twenty first century irrespective of societal modernity through advance educational system, social structure based on the application of the rule of law and the efficacy of natural justice, political advancement and institutional development through transportation and communication. In pre-modern time, the level of human civilization was shaded with profound illiteracy, superstition, injustices without any redress which culminated to mob rule or the 'law of the jungle' in which ``might`` prevailed over rational thinking and behaviour. In every justification it could be argued that, pre-modernism was an accident of human history and frailty in which criminality was a way of life for survival. The existentiality of facts about pre-modern society was marked by, mysticism of confused belief system which created irrational thinking and attitude that bedevilled the pathway of life in which criminality stood paramount.

It is rather unfortunate that, the attributes of pre-modern society has found a way in modernism and post-modernist society with, vehement repercussions leaving an indelible in print on the mindset of society that, should have been relatively much peaceful and fully protective against the phase of ancient vandalism and societal diabolism. Far from the reality of what it is suppose to be, the opposite is to be expected as a way of life in this present epoch in which, crime is being institutionalised against the backdrop of race, religion and political hegemony.

Modern constitutions are thus embossed with certain tools to create a balance between subjectivism and objectivism of allegations so that, justice could be dispensed free and fairly without nepotism or favouritism. Unlike in the days of old, the dispensation of justice and the philosophy of it were based on subjective views in which, innocent people were victimized by the system that ought, to have protected them.

The philosophy of modernism and post-modernism of crime can be explained within, the concepts of societal and biologically blood related theory. The concept of learning social theory, as a motivating factor of most criminal offences, tend to examined what happened in society that influences our behaviour towards criminality. It is argued by exponents of social theory that, the way society is structured, depict behaviour. If for instance, society is institutionally corrupt via the legislator, executive and the judiciary; poverty and deprivation with national health crises will tend to systemically occur through ant-social behaviour of crime and deviance. Since irresponsible government produces, reckless and unaccountable executive and the judiciary, it couldn't be a surprise to connote the negative impact it will have on society.

On the other hand, those who expostulates the biological theory of behaviour argued that, blood connection has much to do with behaviour and that social structure is just a part of it but not holistically. Thus they argued that, irrespective of the political and socio-economic structure of society, some people will tend to tilt their behaviour pattern decently within the parameters of the law. Those they argued who engaged in acts of criminality could have had connection by blood to a family before them, obnoxious of anti-social behaviour and crime. In this scenario, the exponents of biological concept injected the phrase of ``**dog produces dog and snakes do snakes**''. **Although this phrase adage could be limited to modernistic advancement in science and technology of biological mutation of species yet, it is not far from reality that, such could reasonably be the case.**

It is against this backdrop that, the principle law and morality under the concept of **jurisprudence** is very essential in the dispensation of free and fair justice. Common law which tend to dictate principles of law in its' entirety with some element of harshness is always, balanced on a scale of morality of equity in which, characteristics/ behaviour of accused persons are taken into cognisance in the deliberation of justice especially in criminal law. For the purpose of understanding, the following example of are of essence:

Sample A: in this scenario, **y** is accused of rape and was brought to court where his past behaviour was investigated and found to be very good and cordial with profound respectability for people. He was also found to be honest, gentle, and helpful with no history of criminal record and abuse case. It was also discovered that following thorough investigation that, the victim did hypnotise and seduced the accused by being naked before him, creating an open invitation for action. In delivering the verdict, the judge, after perusing the accused behavioural past in juxtaposition of the reality of the incident, equity was immediately applied which reduces the burden of imprisonment on the accused.

It is thus established that, those who wish to use equity to soften the harshness of common law, must do so with clean hands or else, equity could not be applied.

CHAPTER EIGHT

Part Two

Under this section few cases will be high-lighted in synopsis so that, awareness as to how, judges and other legal adjudicators, in legally constituted courts, arrived at their verdicts in certain case scenarios. An examination will also be made in certain areas of legal conflicts between common law and equity and how certain verdicts are nullified by the decisions of the Law Lords in the House of Lords.

Since it is not possible to cover the entire field of case law, students are advised to read up other cases as to when and where possibly necessary in the bid to enhancing own personal skills.

However, much ground could be covered to enhancing the appetite and desire of students wishing to studying law and to gradually building self confidence and enthusiasm of having law as their choosing career.

Cases that are mentioned in this section of the book are not in any particular order but rather randomly selected for the purpose of recapitulation exercises. This in any way does not reduce the importance of what those cases had been at the time of adjudication.

Finally, it should be noted that, these cases shall be paraphrased to avoid duplicity and boredom which are usually fashionable with case laws.

STEP1. In looking at cases within the ambit of the law, it is but highly essential, to briefly discuss what sort of cases that goes to Crown court and those that are, meant for Magisterial court within the English legal system. Basically speaking, Magistrate court is also known as Justices of the Peace, which usually tried cases of lesser sentences and usually held by a district judge who is a lawyer in most cases. Cases of higher magnitude such as murder, rape, arson and rubbery are dealt with at the Crown Court being duly referred to such court by the Magisterial Jurisdiction that hasn't the legal power to handle such cases.

CASE A: Abusive Husband
R V Kanagusobi Ramanathan

In the years that followed their marriage, a 73 year old woman was duly cleared of murder, after years of repeated abused from her deceased husband. According to the facts of the case, the accused who was looking after a disabled husband, had constantly abused her to such levity that she decided finally to extricate herself of such gross inhuman abuse by blotting him with a club severally on the head as he laid asleep on the bed.

Stephen Komlish QC, appearing for the defendant, argued that, if Mrs Romanathan, had wanted to intentionally killed her disabled husband, she could have done so quickly and wittingly by an over dose of insulin she administered to her for the past years without any trace of evidence. He therefore directed the jury to take note of the fact that, since she didn't do what most victims of such depraved circumstances could have done, it follows no intention to killed and thus directed the jury to return a none guilty verdict. When members of the jury went to deliberate on the faith of the aforesaid defendant, it was then unanimously decided that the defendant had indeed endured duress, and even threats to her life and for her to have withstood such pressure for 73 years, clearly indicate exceptional courage and love which any reasonable person couldn't have endured and thus returned a none guilty verdict.

CASE B: Abusive woman
R V Hannegret Donnelly

A woman was found guilty and jailed for murder after haven been abusive of her late husband whose disability gave her an advantage to do what she did. According to the hearing, it was stated that, the accused repeatedly struck her husband, the former music instructor with rolling pin on his head which resulted to a massive blood clothe in the brain which culminated his death. Sentencing the 55 year old retired midwife, the judge told her that, her calculated evil was meant to achieve a decisive success in her murder plan of which she was able to accomplish. After the trial, the police criminal service issued a brief statement saying that; `` at last it is now proven that women could also be capable of abusing men``.

CASE C: **HILL V BAXTER (1958)**

In this case, a stretched to the understanding of Actus Reus and Mens Rea, was put to the legal test as to what usually happened when an absence of a voluntary physical act is questionable in the advent of an offence. Thus in this case, it was stipulated that, when the vehicle was in motion, the driver was stung by a bee on his face and immediately took his hands off the car which resulted into a serious crash. In court, he pleaded not guilty since his physical act of taken his hands off the car, was due to reflection act rather than a calculated act of **Actus Reus. In addition to this, he pleaded that, Mens Rea was never conceived prior to the clash.** In the descending judgement, Lord Goddard, remarked that, at times circumstances could arise when it is not possible to be in control of a desperate situation such as stroke or an epileptic fit which leads to unconsciousness. This he argued to be involuntary in action in which, part of the body seems to be in action without any involvement of the mind and physical application. Thus, both physical and mental application were absent to which none guilty verdict was upheld.

NOTE: The issue in the above case, (Hill V Baxter) is that which deals with certain part of the law that relates to Non Insane automatism. Accordingly, it could be possible for certain acts be devoid of voluntary physical act (Actus Reus) and that of mentally constructive involvement (Mens Rea) no matter the seriousness or magnitude of the offence. For example, at times it is possible for certain parts of the body to be moving without, the awareness of the brain as to what the body is doing. This is what may be termed as Reflex action which is entirely involuntary. Sleeping walking could be an example of this. Also, people that suffers from depression, epileptic fit all constitute area of concern by the government as to best it could endeavoured to create a balance between their adverse action against innocent victims of society in the pursuit of their human right violation. In order words, how can people or any accused person uses Non Insane automatism as defence against punishment when a breach of the law on the other hand is highly prognostic. In most cases certain prevailing situation, doesn't allow an accused person to use Non Insane automatism as defence to escape punishment because of what could be connected to their sense of responsibility under duty of care. For example, if a driver suddenly fall asleep while driving that leads to a fatal accident, such a driver can not apply the term, Non Insane automatism as defence since he is under duty of care to drive safely and by putting the safety of passengers and other road users as his optimum concern. Tiredness is natural but can be controlled and is controllable which means that, the tired driver could have realised this by stopping for a rest but choose to take chances to the detriment of those he recklessly victimized.

SEE: Kay V butterworth (1945)

CHAPTER NINE

Step: 2

Under this chapter, a brief discussion on situational liability will be examined as to whether it falls within the ambit of criminal offence in which, proof of the **Actus Reus** can be justifiable where such is to be perused within the law. In order words, it is required to prove that, something was actually done physically to justify criminal offence. One of the difficulties in criminal litigation is to be able to logically and legally prove that the nature of the mind-set is in complete relation or concurrently in tuned with the physical act. The question is; if the mind-set is not connected to the physical act, should criminal liability be established? An examination of some of these can to some extent, gives clues as to which way criminality could be best explained.

Winzar V Chief Constable of Kent (1938)

In this case, a man was found copiously drunk within the hospital premises by the police. He was told to leave but refused to do so and as such, was forcefully removed and put into the police van and driven. He was put down on the roadside and was simultaneously arrested for being drunk on the highway. Even though he was physically found on the highway yet, he never anticipated within his mind to be there.

Although the accused never intended to have been on the highway yet, situational circumstances militated against him to have being guilty of the act.

R V Nicholls (1874)

Where it is established that a person had accepted responsibility of duty of care of human creature which results into wicked negligence, culminating to death of the aforesaid human, such person shall be guilty of Manslaughter.

Seemingly, if a person creates a dangerous situation it becomes imperative for such person to help resolve the situation or else, shall be guilty of criminal liability. An example of such situation is that which could be examined under **R V Miller (1983).** In this case the accused went to bed without putting out the cigarette he was smoking which caught fire on the mattress he was sleeping. Upon waking up, he did nothing to put out the fire but rather simply, went into another room to continue sleeping. The entire was engulf into flame and had to escape to save his life. The vagrant was later charged for arson and was found guilty of criminal liability. in the descending judgement of Lord Diplock, it was clearly stipulated that; any conduct which is capable of creating criminal liability of which such conduct lies within the power of the person to stop or prevent such act but failed to doing so, should constitutes an act of serious criminal liability for a guilty verdict.

Another area of law under criminal liability which is essential to be examined with reasonable caution is **Novus Actus Interveniens.** At times victims of circumstantial act could be responsible for what may or could have happened to them. In order words, those who suffered as a result of another person's act shall themselves be responsible for the aforesaid outcome.

SEE: R V Blaue (1975), R V Holland (1841) and R V Marjoram (200)

In all of these cases, it is advisable to be cautious while making a presentation on the basis of current material facts which couldn't have been available at the material time those cases were tried. In order words, what was an acceptable law upon which most of those mentioned cases were based could be refuted if it is to be retried in the age of modernism and post-modernism.

In criminal litigation, there can be indirect causation which when it is successfully established, give rise to prosecution. Although several cases have been cited to reasonably, substantial a guilty verdict, yet there is one landmark case which explicitly, give clarity to what happened when causation is indirect.

SEE: Halstead V Chief Constable of Derbyshire (2000).

In this case, T who had a 12 months old baby in her arm, was visited by a former boy friend called D. Although she had told D never to visit her yet when he came to the house, she opened the door for him and upon entry, he punched W on the face which made her to lose her gripe of the child and fell to the floor. D was then prosecuted for Battery and was indicted. In the bid to establishing the cause of death, questions were raised as to whether, the defendant act was sufficiently substantial to have caused the death of the 12 months baby or was his act of punching responsible for the loose of griped on the baby which culminated to the fatal incident. In this scenario, the "**BUT FOR TEST**" was established in examining as to whether in the absence of the punching, the 12 months old baby would have fell to such fatality. After much deliberations, it was held that, hadn't it being for the act of the defendant, the incident which occurred wouldn't have happened. In this regard, it was held that, defendant was guilty for indirectly causing death of the child because his action thought not have intended, did result to the demised of the child.

Secondly, it was held that, defendant, would have foreseen that, his vagrant and brutal action against T in her given situation was going to produce an ugly and fatal result and nevertheless, blatantly went ahead to execute his ego. In this regard, the **Foreseeability Test** was also applied in Torts Law in which it is held that, the action of the defendant was adequately sufficient and substantial to establish injury to the innocent patty or victim. Had D realised that an innocent child was in a much vulnerable situation should he acted the way he did, he would have aborted his action against W for the safety of the child. Because he went ahead to do what he did, realising that fatality will result, both Torts and common law could by and large, militate against him for any defence to extricate himself acquitter.

CHAPTER TEN

In this chapter, the issue of Torts Law will be examined within the parameters of duty of care as legal obligation. First, it will be examined whether, omission or failure to act, constitute an offence especially where it is reasonably foreseeable that, such failure or omission could by and large, lead to injury to another person. In order words, should legal liability be established in a situation where, a person's failure to act result to injury to another innocent victim who should have been protected or saved if intervention had not been withheld.

In English Torts Law, an individual will be liable for the protection of another person and failure to act, in circumstances where harm is likely possible then such, shall be liable under the law for compensation to the victim. Simple question to this scenario is whether Doctors' have duty of care to their patients whom they are medically looking after. If this is the case, should legal responsibility be levelled against any of such a breach if it occurs? Attempting answers to such questions, it is essential to elucidate some legal cases for clarity of understanding as follows:

CASE A
Michael V Croydon Health Services -2018 (NHS)

In 2018, a situation arose where the victim had a severe head injury and was rushed to the above A&E department of the above hospital. Upon arrival, he was told by the receptionist that he will have to wait for 4-5 hours. The victim's friend who assisted him to the hospital, pleaded that his friend will collapse if he was to have waited all that time. In response, the receptionist said that, the victim will be considered for emergency consideration if he collapsed within the stipulated time frame. In view of this, the victim's friend decided to take him to his mother of which upon arrival, he collapsed just within 4-5 hours. Matters arising from this issue was, whether, the hospital should be responsible under duty of care for the victim.

Jackson L J acting on behalf of the defendant, argued that, no duty of care is owed to the victim for the fact that, when the victim was told about 4-5 hours waiting time, did not constitute any legal liability if collapsed was to have happened outside the hospital premises of which it did. He went on to argue that, had the victim waited within the premises of the hospital, any collapse, would have been treated as an emergency under duty of care. It was further argued that, damage to the victim was outside the description of the hospital environment to which, no logical reference could be established in creating a causal link to justify breach in any aforesaid duty of care. Therefore, it was stated that, when the appellant told the defendant about the specificity of time duration for medical treatment, no anticipation of duty of care was envisaged especially outside the hospital environment.

This was overturned by the Supreme Court when Lord Lloyd Jones under paragraph 16 argued that, this case was under an established law of duty of care with absolutely no change which means that, the defence had failed in his attempt to establish, a new law on duty of care. He went on to say that, duty of care as established under Torts Law has not changed and cannot be substituted with another unrecognised case law.

In his closing argument, he clearly and categorically stated that, by allowing the patient upon arrival at the receptionist desk to have registered, a duty of care was established between the hospital staff and that of the victim and friend, this he went on to say that, created a duty of care that cannot be substituted by the assumption of another duty of care which is none existent for the purpose of legal argument. **(See Barnett V Chelsea and Kensington hospital).**

Seemingly, Lord Lloyd Jones expostulated that, the victim's reliance on the misleading advice of the hospital receptionist, brought him to a situation that could have been avoided. Applying the Caparo case test scenario, three possible legal questions were raised such as; whether, the injury or harm was reasonably foreseeable, whether the parties involved were in relationship before the harm and finally whether the treatment was fair and just. **(See Caparo Industries V Dickman etel)**

In addition to this, Lord Atkin in his approached on duty of care put forward a 'Neighbour Test' in which he argued that, duty of care is owed to each other and any breach in such duty, constitute negligence and lack of duty of care which constitute a serious offence. **(See Donoghue Stevenson's case)**

When the receptionist at the Croydon hospital (NHS Trust) was advising the victim and is friend who took him to the E&A Department of the hospital, did any recklessness of behaviour on the part of the receptionist established. Basically, when the receptionist took such decision to advice on the related hours of emergency treatment, an unjustifiable risk was simply taking which could be related to a person taking a stupid risk of crossing a traffic light before it goes ''green''.

Recklessness of any description is a criminal offence which the law takes seriously. In this regard, it will be necessary to elucidate the two approaches in dealing with recklessness within the framework of criminal litigation under negligence and lack of duty of care. The victim's lawyer was able to argue further that, the action of the receptionist was tantamount to subjective recklessness because it was reasonably foreseeable that someone was going to be injured. **In**

R V Cunningham (1957) an accused stole money from a gas meter by ripping off the meter from the wall which made copious gas escaped that poisoned innocent people. He was accused of subjective recklessness because he knew his action was going to cause, harm to innocent people.

Also, a person could be guilty under lack of duty of care for criminal damages under S1 (1) of the 1971 criminal damage Act if such behaviour was to cause damages to property that is foreseeable to be the case. In **R V Caldwell (1982),** a guest who was very unhappy with the owner of the hotel set fire on the property with damaging consequences. Under this scenario an objective recklessness was established in which according to Lord Diplock's argument constitute criminal damages against the background that, the action of the defendant does creates an obvious risk to the hotel but was never deterred rather, went ahead to do what should have been avoided. Although this part of the argument is unrelated to the Croydon hospital incident yet, it also indicates how recklessness under lack of duty of care could result to criminal damages.

CHAPTER ELEVEN

Epilogue

Criminality and punishment, tend to be, the yardstick or social barometer upon which much academic debates and intellectual discourse have been, pivoted by various geopolitical system of governments in the bid to creating and establishing a just, fair, prudent, humane and truly representative organs of government for the dignity and preservation of human civilization devoid of social barbarism in an attempt to curb vagrant and other diabolic antisocial behaviour tantamount to, civil unrest.

Before the epoch of modern and pre-modern society, criminality was considered a very serious capital offence which had no objective judicial trial. Accused persons were liable to face the full force of punishment without any due process of legal systemic investigation as it is done today. During the periods of the 15/16 centuries, crime was a stigmatization of social stench which, has to be rebelled against by punitive measures of capital death related punishment even, where such, wasn't called for. Those who were accused of being witches and wizards, were without due process of legal proceedings burnt alive in public and those who were accused of stealing in market places exposed to death seemingly.

What should be noted is that, during this period, it was likely possible for miscarriage of justice to occur since, accused persons were not given the opportunity to defend themselves within the parameters of the **Rule of Law** as it is today. Victimization of innocent persons, who could be suspected of haven opposite opinion of the system or critical of the authority's style of administration, could be easily accused of being a threat to society and put to death even though, in reality such threat never could have existed.

It was not a surprise to realised how, a fragrant violation of human right was constantly maintained unchallenged in lure of the fact that, those who were meant to defend justice, were corrupt and viciously addicted to power and could go 'extra miles' to implement policies capable of militating against fundamental human right.

Criminality during those periods (15/16 centuries) was considered a social construct in which it was felt and argued that, crime had to do with, the way in which society was patterned on the basis of family structure/ organization. Crime therefore, is a "family disease" which had been deeply rooted and therefore, can't be easily eradicated by simple gesture of lenient approach except on the basis of corrosiveness and ruthlessness of action. In this regard, some families were labelled as prone to criminality and as such, any information of social unrest, crime, and other related offences could be directed immediately to such targeted families to which due process following arrest, will be unnecessary other than, straight forward imprisonment and execution.

This ideology of crime related family was extended to include race, religion, ethnicity, traditional values, and belief system. It is the more reason why, in our modern and pre-modern societies, criminality is defined and viewed as situated within certain race, religion, ethnicity and belief system which has to be dealt with punitively without due process.

In certain part of Africa society, some tribes, race and cultural values, were considered as mere threat to the peace and stability of the society and thus, has to be brutalised with impunity. In the West, this barbaric and uncivilised behaviour, laid the foundation of the two great wars which found expression in the extermination of countless millions of people. In Asia and the Far East, an adumbration of injustice and mass victimizations are common practice in violation of the basic fundamental human right. In the United States of America, irrespective of its' vast and complex system, criminality is still viewed as a `race thing` since the time of certain great human right activists like Luther King (junior)and others.

The question is, why should crime be, racially related or why is it that certain people are deemed as, criminals because of their racial background or religious make-up even though in most cases, such assumptions could be misleading and therefore out of place.

Why should people get involved in criminal activities; in order words, why should people become attracted to crime? Over the years, social theorists, have made several attempts to explain why this is the case using different hypothetical approaches such as, societal and biological factors as the main motivating reasons for their criminality. Those social theorists who purported the ideology of social influence, argued that, it is the nature of society, its systemic structure and organization in classifying people within the whims of the ``haves`` and they ``have not``, culminate a strange philosophy of ``we the left-out and the marginalised are compelled to maintained respectable existence at all cost irrespective of outcome``.

Those who believe in the biological approach, argued that, society and the influence of peer group, has no effective ground to sustained and justify criminality except through the orientation of ``blood connection``. Those who are unfortunate to have been conceived in criminal oriented family nexus shall be prone to criminality irrespective of their class positions. Those, who are criminals, are biologically predisposed to be. They exponents went on to say that, societal influence and structure has nothing to do with criminality related- behaviour. In order words, those who were born in a criminal family or a family with prolific police criminal records shall unquestionably become prone to criminality.

Against this background, any law that has been drafted and put in place to deal with crime, always rest on the platform of ``state of mind `` prior to action and the ``physical act`` itself.

The principle of separation of power, rule of law, independence of the judiciary and the human right act of 1988, all constituted to establishing systemic structure based on rational justice as compared to what used to be obtainable in the 15the and 16the centuries.

All accused persons are first deemed innocent until later proven guilty by a duly constituted court before sentencing is pronounced. Accused persons are no longer subjected to jail terms on the basis of their racial background, class position or blood related family nexus until it is been sufficiently and legally proven beyond all reasonable doubt that, such was the case. Any verdict which is based on own wisdom or personal feelings, are subject to an appeal by the accused person. Under this notion, it is constitutionally established that, no one is above the law and that, no one should be arrested without warrant or without being told what offenses they have committed. Seemingly, no one shall be under custody of the police for more than required by the constitution of the aforesaid country. All arrested persons are entitled to legal representation irrespective of social class position meaning that, those who are not able to financially meet the cost of legal representation, are assisted by the state through the Crown Prosecution Service as it in the United Kingdom of Great Britain.

Analysis in the closing chapter of this book is been subjectively put and as a result, readers/ students, are advised to apply self intuition especially where controversy is spotted. It is my expectation that, materials in this book shall enhance the appetite of students wishing to study law to be more inclined to it.

Finally, it is expected that, those who shall be reading this book, could be in the vantage position to understand its simplistic format especially, where basic application of criminal offences are discussed at reasonable length to creating a field of snappy understanding

SIMPLISTIC LEGAL TERMINOLOGIES

(a) Treason: this is a very serious criminal offence against a legally constituted sovereign or state which usually in most countries, attracts the death penalty

(b) Felony: this juxtaposes with treason as very serious offence that attract the death penalty. For example, any act or statement made by individual or group of people that threatens the stability and security of a legally constituted sovereign culminates felonious offence.

(c) Forgery: any act of counterfeiting or falsification of signature on any documentation, constitute a criminal offence punishable by prison terms

(d) Fraud: in juxtaposition with forgery, fraud is any behaviour which is intended to benefit the deceiver against his or her victims. For instance, if a man pretends to be what he is not, and as a result gain out of that deception, fraud is construed accordingly.

(e) Habeas corpus: this is an Act in the English constitution which democratically allowed for any accused person to be under a legal Writ which allows him/her, to be deemed innocent in the phase of any offence until, proven guilty in a legally constituted court based on fair indictable trial

(f) Recidivism: this is when ex-convicts relapse into crime after imprisonment.
(g) Remand prisoners: those prisoners who are in custody awaiting trials. The question is, does this constitute a violation of Human Right?
(h) Pillory: this was a form of criminal punishment in which, accused persons are positioned in a wooden frame for the public to see for couple of weeks which was aimed at shaming the accused.
(i) Embezzlement: this constitutes a serious criminal offence when an individual or group of people divert monies into their accounts without the expressed consent of the owner of the money.
(j) Benefit of the belly: pregnant women who are convicted of criminal offence but, are allowed to be out of punishment until after delivery. This is subject to geo- constitutional structures since, variations in global constitutional structures, differs.

BIBLIOGRAPHY

1. 7McLintock et al Crime in England and Wales (London 1968).
2. McLynn, F. Crime and punishment in the seventeenth and eighteenth century (Oxford, 1989, 1991).
3. Sharpe, J.A. Judicial punishment in England (1990).
4. Carson, W. G. White-collar crime and the institutionalisation of ambiguity et al (London, 1981).
5. Morris, T. Crime and criminal justice since 1945 (Oxford, 1989).
6. Wiener, M. J. Reconstructing the criminal: culture, law, and policies in England 1830- 1914 (Oxford, 1990).
7. Addy, J. Sin and society in the seventeenth century (London, 1989).
8. Bellamy, J. Crime and public order in middle ages (London and Toronto, 1973).
9. Ingram, M. Church courts, sex and marriage in England, 1570-1640 (Cambridge, 1987).
10. Marchant, R.A. The church under the law (Cambridge, 1969).
11. John Briggs et al, Crime and punishment in England (UCL Press London, 1996).
12. Michael, J. Allen, Criminal Law Eight Edition (Sweet& Maxwell London Ltd, 2001).
13. Glazebrook, P. R. Statutes on criminal law (Oxford University Press, 2004-2005)
14. Joel Samaha, Criminal law Twelve Edition (Wandsworth Publishing, 2016).
15. Reneta Lawson Mack, layperson's guide to criminal law (Greenwood Press, 1999).

16. Carl, S. L. The limits of criminal law (Routledge, 2016)
17. Douglas, H. Over-criminalization (Oxford University Press, 2008).
18. George, P. F. Rethinking criminal law (Oxford University Press 2000).
19. Norma, L. Law, Crime and English society, 1660-1830 (Cambridge University Press, 2002).
20. Paul H. R. Structure and function in criminal law (Clarendon Press, 1997).

www.ingramcontent.com/pod-product-compliance
Lightning Source LLC
Chambersburg PA
CBHW031540210526
45464CB00003B/1082